THE ROBIN AND THE RAVEN

MY WOUNDED FRIEND

An allegory based upon a **"true story"** portrayed in two birds and two best friends. Both experienced a tragedy in their lives and found hope through a miracle when they least expected it.

Written by Robin Elaine Baldwin
(Story is given by the inspiration of the Holy Spirit)
(May 28, 2012-2016)

P.O. Box 50012, Bowling Green, KY 42102
StandingStoneMinistries@gmail.com
RobinandTheRaven@gmail.com

Illustrations by John T. Simpson

ACKNOWLEDGEMENTS

This book is dedicated to my "Shepherd."
Thank you God for setting me free from my sin.
The bird fowler (hawk bird) had set many traps for me, and Jesus has
delivered me from each one. You watch over me, and keep me safe. You
are my life savior, rescuer, and the Good Shepherd. Jesus, You are the
Savior of the World, and thank You for Your abiding love. (Psalm 91)
My Teacher, Counselor and Friend. Jesus said, "Greater love has no
one than this, than to lay down one's life for his friends."
(John 14:26, John 15:13)

This story is dedicated to Bobby "bird"
God's deep love for you is the reason this story exist.
Thank you for the many years of loving, learning and growing together.
Our joys and trials together have made me a better person.
Bobby, I love you more than life itself. I thank God for you!
You are forever in my heart, for you are a treasure.

Special Thanks

Thank you Margie, for your friendship and prayers. In the writing of this book, God placed you in my life exactly when it was needed. You're an inspiration to me through your encouraging words, love and support. Your family has been an inspiration to me as well, especially your sister Kathy and your nephew John. Thank you Kathy for your patience, encouragement, and support for your son John, in the preparation of these illustrations for the book. Thank you John for using your God-given artistic abilities and willingness to illustrate. You are a dear young man that God is using in a mighty way. As you continue to glorify His name with your talent, you will be blessed.

PREFACE

This is a true story, written in an allegory form, about my dear

friend, whom I love more than life itself,

and how brokenness and a snare separated us for a short season.

This story is about faith, hope, and love,

reconciliation, and redemption.

God used a true event of two birds to show us His

compassion and mercy for His wounded children.

INTRODUCTION

The real life event that inspired the book

One day while I was walking my dog Shiloh near our home, I saw two ravens. One raven was flying in the air frantically, making all kinds of noise, while the other raven was caught in a fence with a broken wing. I stopped and stood still watching this unfold. To my sadness, this beautiful black bird was caught in the snare of the fence and could not fly to safety. He was frighten, and confused as was the other raven who was flying overhead.

From my prospective, the airborne raven seem to feel helpless for her companion caught in the fence. They both seem to be in a place of despair and disbelief. I felt their pain and fear and I desperately wanted them to be free. Strangely enough I could do nothing but watch and pray for their story to end well. I could relate, because I was in a similar situation with my best friend. I was feeling helpless with no way to fix what was broken in their life or mine.

This true life event of the two ravens at the pond parallels to the story in the book, "The Robin and the Raven, My Wounded Friend." Both the event of the ravens and my own personal story are similar in nature. As their tragedy was underway, mine would begin to unfold within the next year. The day of the ravens, an impression came to me, that one day I would write a book on this day's event.

The story, The Robin and the Raven, is about two birds, who became best friends, and built their life together. However, later in the friendship a tragedy hits when they least expect it. What they will discover is how to depend upon God for help.

This has been a long season of waiting on the Lord, praying, believing and trusting. But nothing is wasted with God, He uses everything to grow us.

The Bible tells us to be strong and courageous, and do not be afraid. It tells us that God will never leave or forsake us who believe in Him. The LORD Himself goes before us and will be with us every step of the way.
(Deuteronomy 31:6, 8)

God is able to come and rescue us from any trauma or tragedy we may encounter in life. All we need to do is ask in prayer, believe He will do it, then trust Him with it.

> "Those who wait on the Lord,
> Shall renew their strength;
> They shall mount up with wings like eagles,
> They shall run and not be weary,
> They shall walk and not faint."
> (Isaiah 40:31)

This story is a lesson of humility, and trusting God to do only what He can do. Brokenness should humble us, because only a mighty God can deliver us. Only Jesus can save, heal, restore, and redeem. Out of the darkness came a great Light. (Isaiah 9:2)

Jesus said, "If you believe, you will receive whatever you ask in prayer." Matthew 21:22

CONTENTS

CHAPTER 1

One Beautiful Day...

One beautiful day in August, a robin bird came to play in the lush green meadows of Barren River Lake.

At the lake there were swans, meadow larks, cardinals, robins, and sparrows too. Some birds were having fun playing in the water, while others were flying around in the trees making fine feathered friends. However there was this one particular bird that caught robin bird's eye. It was a black bird and his feathers were not ordinary; "His head had locks that were bushy, and black as a raven." (Song of Solomon 5:11)

As the robin bird watched the black bird, she noticed this was a sensitive bird and quite handsome. The black bird knew how to sing, and he used his instrument to attract attention. Robin bird said to herself, *"I'd like to get to know him."*

Robin bird asked around with the other birds, but no one seem to know who the black bird was, or where he was from. However, she kept an eye on him from a distance, but was intrigued with him none the less.

The end of the Beautiful Day was coming to a close. The sun was waving goodbye with a beautiful orange glow upon the lake. Robin bird saw that evening was drawing near, so robin bird said to herself, *"It is time to fly back home."* As robin bird gathered her feathers, she looked over at the tree next to hers and saw the lonely black bird with the beautiful wavy feathers becoming silent. She noticed his singing had become more subdued, as he watched robin bird prepare to fly home.

Friends Forever...

The summer sun rose early the next day, as robin bird decide she wanted to go to town where the "Singing Station" was.

Robin bird loved the singing station, it's where birds of a feather flock together to sing songs on a live wire.

Robin bird approached the singing station, and out of the corner of her eye, she saw something black. To her surprise, it was the black bird she saw at the lake the day before.

Robin bird saw the black bird was coming to perch in a nearby tree. Then black bird said to robin bird, *"Hi, I'm a raven, but you can call me bobby bird. What are you?"* "Robin bird replied, *"I'm a robin bird."*

The robin and the raven struck up a conversation that lasted for days. They had a grand ole time becoming friends, and they had many things in common. They loved to sing, talk, and play in the trees, which was next to the pond, near their nest.

Their friendship included gathering food, straw and twigs, for making their nest together. It seemed nothing could ever upset this wonderful friendship that God put together, until one day something happened.

CHAPTER 2

One Cloudy Day...

One Cloudy Day both robin bird and bobby bird were heading to the pond near their nest for a day of fun. Then swiftly a big *red-eyed hawk* bird came flying fast and furious towards them. The hawk swooped down and hit bobby bird so hard, he knocked him out of the air.

Bobby bird landed on his back, at the fence and was wounded. When robin bird saw this, she became fearful and kept circling around and around trying to figure out how to help her best friend. Robin bird didn't know what to do. She had never seen something like this happen before, and she knew bobby bird was in a bad way.

Robin bird cried out to bobby bird, *"Are you okay? Can you fly?"* But bobby bird didn't answer a word. The raven had the wind knocked out of him, and he was trying to right himself from the hit. He kept trying to use his wing, but it would not move, it was broken. His pain was so great, with every attempt to escape the snare the raven dug himself in deeper and deeper into the fence.

The raven bird needed help, he was no longer in control of his life. Robin bird was concerned for her best friend, she did not know what to do. All she could do was watch and cry out for help to anyone who would listen. Sadly, nobody was listening.

While bobby bird laid helpless, robin bird went round and round in circles, trying to reason this out. She tried so hard in her strength, but could not help bobby bird. The more she tried, the more fearful she became until she was useless in helping bobby bird. They were both afraid.

The Snare...

Robin bird became sad because the fence bobby bird had fallen into had ensnared him in its grip. (2 Timothy 2:26, Psalm 91:3)

Robin bird thought, "What can I do?"

Days had passed and now both birds had given up trying to fix what neither could fix, they both were in a mess. Bobby bird was laying there not able to get up out of the snare. Robin bird could not seem to gather herself from the fear of losing her best friend. They both felt helpless with each passing day.

One day, robin bird decided to call upon several bird friends for help. However, they did not know how to help, so they just flew on by.

Robin bird decided to pull bobby bird from the fence herself, but the more she pulled, and tugged, the more his wing became wounded.

"What can I do?" said robin bird.

Robin bird knew she could not leave her best friend to fend for himself. The snare that was set for him made him easy prey for creatures of the night.

Robin bird thought, and thought and thought some more. Robin bird finally said... *"I will have to call on the One who created us for His good pleasure. Maybe He can help us."* **(Philippians 2:13)**

So robin bird cried day and night and prayed to God for help.

CHAPTER 3

The Plan...

The two birds, did not quit! They did not give up praying, they did not give up hope. Their Creator knew that both robin bird and bobby bird found it hard to give up control of fixing their plight. God heard their prayers, and He would send His Helper.

God answered and said....

"I know the thoughts that I think towards you says the Lord... thoughts of peace and not of evil, to give you a future and a hope. I will deliver you from your snare." (Reference Jeremiah 29:11-14)

Upon hearing this, robin bird cried, and bobby bird sighed. For God had a plan for them, not to do harm, but good.

Robin bird liked to plan and reason things out. However, robin bird realized God is in control and she could trust God. Robin bird soon discovered she could not fix or heal her best friend, only God could do that.

Bobby bird realized he could not control his life circumstances. Everything he tried did not work. Bobby bird could not heal himself or get free of the snare his enemy, the hawk set for him. As the robin and the raven waited on God, they prayed together. They became even closer friends than ever before.

The Rescue...

Then one night, an answer came. God, their Creator sent a message in a dream to robin bird. In the dream robin bird saw bobby bird in the "Healing Waters." And all that had ensnared him fell off into the "Waters." In the dream, robin bird saw that bobby bird found peace in the waiting, and he was released from everything that had bound him. (John 5:4, John 7:38-39)

Early the next morning as the sun was rising, a sweet dew was on the ground, and a crisp-cool breeze was stirring. Robin bird awoke from her dream. She was so excited, that she could hardly wait to tell bobby bird about the dream and the healing waters. However, as robin bird was coming down from her perch, she saw a Shepherd who had many sheep coming bobby bird's way. Robin bird waited patiently to see what was happening with the Shepherd.

The good Shepherd came to where the raven bird was laying on the ground. He saw he was wounded and caught in the snare of the fence. Bobby bird was not able to move, he had become exhausted from the entanglement of the snare. So many days had passed since the fall. Bobby bird had kicked up a lot of dirt from his self efforts to free himself. It had been a long hard fight, but now help had come.

The good Shepherd carefully picked up the wounded raven. The raven did not make a sound, because the Shepherd's hand was gentle. The Shepherd carefully cleansed the dirt and debris from the bird. Then He wrapped him in a soft white cloth. He carefully put the raven next to His heart for safe keeping.

The robin bird seeing that the good Shepherd was there to help, breathed with a sigh of relief. The robin was grateful to God for sending His Rescuer in her hopes of healing her best friend, bobby bird, the raven.

The Lord is my Shepherd, He restores my soul. (Psalm 23)

That day, the Shepherd added the little black bird to His flock. He took him back to His house for a time of restoration and wellness. Robin bird was so happy, she flew around and around with great joy. She was no longer impatient, for help had finally arrived. God sent the Shepherd to save her best friend from the snare of the fence. In robin bird's long waiting, her faith and trust in God grew. The One who created them for His good pleasure had come.

The good Shepherd had a plan for this beautiful black bird, the raven. He created him with the black wavy feathers, who was sensitive in nature.

The Shepherd cleansed, and healed the Raven and brought him back to life. The raven was well, the good Shepherd released him to the beautiful meadow and lake. He was no longer wounded, or afraid.

The robin and the raven and their feathered friendship is better than ever before. The raven's way with words and song are filling the heavenlies once again. Bobby bird said to God the Creator...

"Lord watch between me and robin bird while we are apart."
(Genesis 31:40)

God keeps watch while we are apart from those whom we love. Robin bird kept a birds eye view on bobby bird. However God's eye never left bobby bird, not even for a second. God keeps His promises. God sent His Rescuer, just when all seemed lost.

The Big Party...

There was a big party, and birds of a different feather flock together and celebrated with robin bird, and bobby bird. Now both birds are singing a new song, and dancing a new dance, and hold feather to feather in their Creator's Care.

Both the robin and the raven had a need for a Rescuer,
a Savior, the good Shepherd. Their friendship alone
was not enough to fix their fears, hurts or wounds.

Jesus sticks closer than a friend, closer
than a brother, even closer than feather to
feather. Pray and believe, trust in Jesus.
He will deliver you from your snare, your hurt, your pain.
Jesus cares for you.
To God be the Glory!

The End

About the Illustrator

John T. Simpson, Illustrator

John loves art! He has been an artist all of his life, even as a very young boy. Though he has explored a variety of mediums, watercolor is his favorite. Portraiture is his specialty. John lives in Kentucky with his family.

Bibliography

Biblical Scripture References
Scripture based upon The New King James Version, unless otherwise noted.

Psalm 91, John 14:26, John 15:13, Deuteronomy 31:6, 8, Isaiah 40:31, Isaiah 9:2, Matthew 21:22, Song of Solomon, 5:11, 2 Timothy 2:26, Psalm 91:3, Philippians 2:13, Jeremiah 29:11-14, John 5:4, John 7: 38-39, Psalm 23, Genesis 31:40. Other Reference: Ezekiel 47:9

Bird Fun Facts

Noah used a raven to test the flood waters for dry ground. (Genesis 8:7). Ravens were sent by God to feed one of His prophets, Elijah. (1 Kings 17:6). "The Raven are among the smartest of all birds. Gaining a reputation of solving ever more complicated problems by ever more creative scientist. They are always looking for a quick meal, and therefore these big sooty birds thrive on being around humans." www.allaboutbirds.org

"The Robin sings the most beautiful tune and is often the last bird heard just before the sun sets and the first one before sun rise. Robin's have a sweet tooth. They love fruits, berries and sweet cakes, and even pastry dough are their favorites. When Robins are feeding in flocks, they are a vigilant bird, and watches other birds reactions to predators." www.birdfeeders.com   www.wikipedia.org

The Robin and the Raven, "My Wounded Friend,"

Scripture taken from the New King James Version®. Copyright © 1982 by Thomas Nelson. Used by permission. All rights reserved.

WestBow Press books may be ordered through booksellers or by contacting:

WestBow Press
A Division of Thomas Nelson & Zondervan
1663 Liberty Drive
Bloomington, IN 47403
www.westbowpress.com
1 (866) 928-1240

Because of the dynamic nature of the Internet, any web addresses or links contained in this book may have changed since publication and may no longer be valid. The views expressed in this work are solely those of the author and do not necessarily reflect the views of the publisher, and the publisher hereby disclaims any responsibility for them.

Any people depicted in stock imagery provided by Thinkstock are models, and such images are being used for illustrative purposes only.
Certain stock imagery © Thinkstock.

ISBN: 978-1-5127-7621-8 (sc)
ISBN: 978-1-5127-7622-5 (e)

Library of Congress Control Number: 2017902624

Print information available on the last page.

WestBow Press rev. date: 01/08/2019

Printed in the United States
By Bookmasters